AF442961

beWITCHed

POETRY COLLECTION

Ronella Hope Segaya

beWITCHed

Ronella Hope Segaya

For the woman dancing with me at nights
my mother would see me
swaying alone

Ronella Hope Segaya, beWITCHed

Not too long ago, maybe a few hundred years back,
I found myself awake from a deep slumber of love.
Travelled mountains, swam oceans and perfect places
Fell into nothingness, counting paces
Sold my soul to the fake sunsets,
I went home with a book printed in my head.
Bid my last goodbye,
Bewitched by
The man, the pain, and the revenge
This collection was the splendid avenge

Ronella Hope Segaya, beWITCHed

Contents

the man

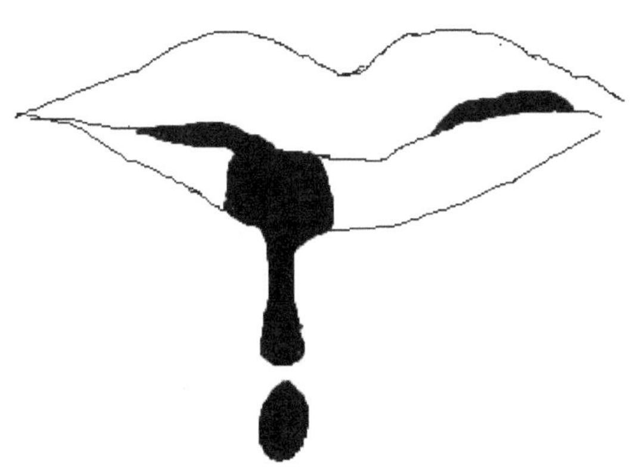

I find you neither under the streetlights of this
expensive city nor inside its proud walls.
You are in the silence of the preying crowd waiting
for my fall.
You are neither the human I welcome inside me
nor the man who claims my body.
You are my veins' romantic poetry.
Bewitch by your magic to send butterflies in my
tummy.

Ronella Hope Segaya, beWITCHed

At the death of what I thought to be the last pain,
blooms new buds of roses.
Darker shade of red this time

Ronella Hope Segaya, beWITCHed

*Give me an idea what
it feels like to be touched
by your fingers and be drowned
by your naked soul.*

Ronella Hope Segaya, beWITCHed

*Love draws
everything but
a straight line.*

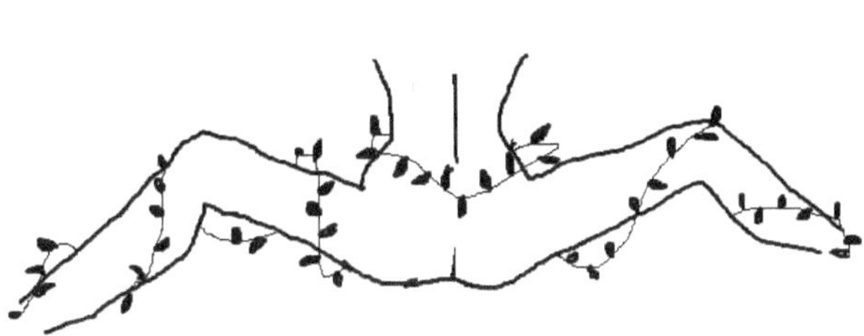

I try so hard not to tell anyone
that you make me want to cut
all the wild leaves that vine my
open legs and close my eyes as
I silently release my prisoners fighting
for forbidden freedom

Ronella Hope Segaya, beWITCHed

You are the fever burning under my skin,
The senseless sense of rush at midnight.
Put your fingers in and defrost my body.
Create fireworks inside me.

Ronella Hope Segaya, beWITCHed

Would you pick my pieces up
when I don't have enough courage
to pick them up?

Would you hang my canvas
when I seemed too short
to hang it myself?

Would you give me
your trust after knowing
I'm too expert at mistrusting?

Would you love me
even I am incapable of loving myself?

Ronella Hope Segaya, beWITCHed

*My demons are begging
me to go astray on the
midnight streets.*

Ronella Hope Segaya, beWITCHed

Imagine my lips on yours,
Tongue-tied in slow motion,
As you touch my cheeks.
You're vibrating in my brain
You can't make me think straight
Never do drugs but with you, I'm high.
Never done this before
Though had several beggings in my pocket
But this is no way near similar
What makes this so different
And confusing but worth trying:
We both are fascinated by ART.

Ronella Hope Segaya, beWITCHed

*I got someone waiting back at home while I walk this midnight street with someone I just met few hours ago. It felt like eternal happiness. It felt like finding peace in a war. It felt like **Shakespeare's** been alive.*

Ronella Hope Segaya, beWITCHed

Look for someone to drive me to the next stop. Undress on highways and paste my body with legs wide open to the stoplight.

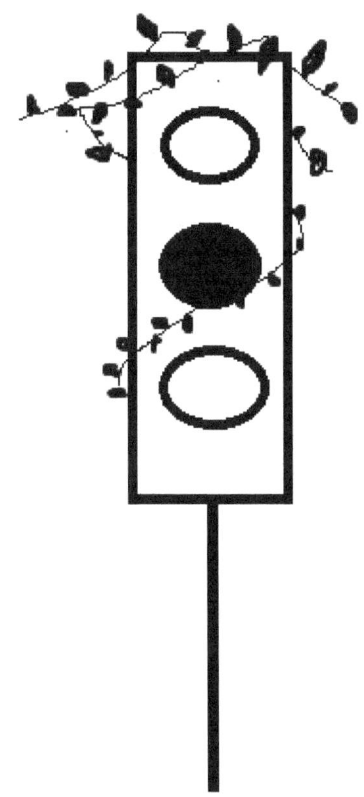

Ronella Hope Segaya, beWITCHed

There is no way
I am selling my body.
I am just dying to know
if how much you would be willing to pay
to touch me.

Ronella Hope Segaya, beWITCHed

Haven't I entered your soul yet?
Am I still an outsider?

Ronella Hope Segaya, beWITCHed

I found a lover beneath my white sheets
Where I hide outline art and poetry
Where freedom knows how fast my cod heart beats
Where sunset disguises its colors for me

I found god in the softness of your lips
Where you say my name and my hair salutes
Where you learn to memorize my wide hips
Where I taste your nakedness, sweet yet pollute

I found the devil smiling in your face
Where I filter thoughts of our long gone days

*I am more than willing
to give you express
ticket to judge my every edge
without hesitation
No matter what are your hidden intentions
This is me offering you a once in a lifetime
opportunity to freedom*

*The freedom to love my flaws that are not
available to everyone*

I'm not supposed to make you my world
But look at me now,
Growing at the mercy of your
Own breathing like you're the only thing that
Could make me grow

Ronella Hope Segaya, beWITCHed

Your honesty satisfies
my every need.
You feed my hunger
for truth and loyalty.

Ronella Hope Segaya, beWITCHed

Let me be your taste test, honey.
I am savoring these little butterflies in my tummy.
I am begging you to be tender with me.
This is a newly found freedom.
This is more than just attaining Socialism.
This is a fresh paradise taking me back to the
pleasure of pain attached to the feeling
of exploring one's self in another yet the same
body.

You are responsible my dear,
To the rebirth of Shakespeare

Ronella Hope Segaya, beWITCHed

*I am no way going for slavery.
However, every atom in my body
wants you to beg for me.*

Ronella Hope Segaya, beWITCHed

You silently watched me unzipped my dress on the midnight streets of this city

And it was the best thing you had ever done for me

Ronella Hope Segaya, beWITCHed

When it comes to you, I run out of words to write. You are a piece of my mind I cannot share with anyone.

Trespass my body,
Screw me, who cares my beloved?
Make sure it feels good.

Whisper me words like,
'I'll stay here beside you' and
You are my only

Caress my thick skin,
Get lost in my curly hair
Take me free of cost

In my fucking art,
You are the most expensive
Word I have written

Be gentle with me,
Allow me to sleep tonight,
I'm all yours honey

Ronella Hope Segaya, beWITCHed

*Sometimes I stare at you
and I can't help but feel
afraid. Someone can't be
too perfect you know?*

Ronella Hope Segaya, beWITCHed

Foreign but welcome. My fingers are cold. My tummy's been screaming wild. My pulse is speeding more than it does. When I am lost for words to write, my lips are dying to say, love. You are making traffic in my veins.

Print my name in your skin, honey. There is no need to escape the red warning. You can expect me not to do the begging but the sensations never stop. It is like Shakespeare's blood is injected to my tunnels and is ready to write again about love. All you have to do is give me a taste of your blood.

Babe, kiss me good night,
As you switch off the red lights,
And wish me sweet dreams

Babe, sneak in your arms
Around my waist, they belong
Listen as I breathe

Babe, promise me this:
When I wake up, you're still here,
'Good morning, sunshine'

Ronella Hope Segaya, beWITCHed

Your walls are up.
I did not know how
fast you rebuilt them.
I just know they're up.

Stay In My Mind

Would it be enough to say that we both just need
someone to talk to,
Or maybe we can try to make an upgrade: tell the
strangers that we meet in the internet, "I love you"
He got a woman sleeping in his bed, he was slowly
fading out of my head, am I writing?
Am I not that smart enough to read and understand
what she meant when she said, "keep the fire burning,"?
All we do is look for the sunrise where money dies while
truth plays unrecognized.
We are wearing the same shoes that we wore through
regardless of the size.
You know I take baits, interrupted base to tunnels and
bottom of the lines.
Who cares if I draw some signs, wrap myself in vines,
and drink you off like wine to take you off my mind?
 Would it be enough to say that I am hungry for honesty
that I saw in you?
Or maybe we can fly to each other's arms and swim the
ocean blue?
He got a girl curling toes as the moon meets Venus in the
starless midnight sky.
I bet she got tattoos on her breasts; your blood is pretty I
guess. Now, they know why.
All we do is look for headlights with wide bind eyes and
try to be headlines tonight.
We can make it the same news that they wrote through
the quarantine lies.
It is foreign, violent rain, beautiful saint, I find.
Who cares if I draw some signs, wrap myself in vines,
and drink you off like wine to take you off my mind?

Ronella Hope Segaya, beWITCHed

Never

Stab my heart as much as you want,
I will never blame you for the pain.
Break the news to everyone:
Tell the universe I am insane.

Strip me naked on the streets,
I will never stop you, darling.
Invite your friends to their seats;
I just hope the stars are watching.

Put the words in my mouth,
I will never shut you out.
Say this girl from the south:
Crowds your brain with fucking doubts

Set the trigger on your finger,
I will never beg you to listen.
Layer your worries on my shoulders,
Try to kiss the strength within

When it is time for you to drop my heart,
I will never judge you, my love
I will never let you know it hurts,
Give you the sweetest smile I have

Ronella Hope Segaya, beWITCHed

This Love: The Lies We Tell

Do they know the prices of things that we sell?
Rites and rights on lies we tell.
Do they know the secrets written, hidden in our faces?
Give birth to this love and fly us to different places.
Do they know the distance between us?
No, they do not know how to focus.
Do they know the speed of this beating in our chest?
Run and crawl, they oversee how we do our bests.

Screaming and pacing, my fingers are shaking.
Tattoo cover the scars, its story is heartbreaking.
Wet pavements and gold cages, we smell like cigarettes.
It is the end of the ages. We chase our silhouettes.
It is time to let them know, babe because they do not know.
The decisive moment and this love will show.
The truth will pave the way for this love to begin.
They will wonder on words we do not even really mean.

Do they know there is freedom on every hours of sleep?
Crashing and wounding our skins but nights, we will rip.
Do they know the fire flowing in our veins?
We are righteous and ber-months birthday saints.
Do they know our arteries are aching and throbbing?
Words of exploitation from the mouth of exploiting
Do they know our intentions and thoughts of yesterday?
They will, now babe because today is the day.

This love is alive. This love is dead.
This love is a fight against death.
This love is pure. This love is false.
This love breaks the widest of the tallest walls.

Ronella Hope Segaya, beWITCHed

FIRST LOVE

First love does not work out, does it?
As I walked down alone at the dark street,
The wet pavements reminded me of something or maybe
someone.

Overdosed with memories I was trying to block out of my
head,
I cut my veins, fought the pain but ended up surrendering at
my bed.
The battles I had to deal on my own, with hopes I ran.

What would make you think of me?
I struggled with thoughts as they brought me to life on
Saturday.
Yet there was no light, neither bird nor sun.

Too strong to hold on to the promises that will never be filled.
For last night, you made up your mind.
You looked ready to destroy and leave me behind.

I hope she loves you more than I do.
Tears escaped my eyes as I packed your things away,
Send them back to you with pictures of our fantasy days.

If I die my love, I hope you know our memories will not.
Burn them, burry or at least send them back to me
Throw them at my door and I will pick them up gently.

If first love does not work out, it is destiny,
Telling us that someone better is waiting at the end of the line
I just hope it is still you with your better self, waiting for me.

If first love does work out, it is destiny,

Ronella Hope Segaya, beWITCHed

Telling us that we are two souls not ready to welcome each other
However, time will only tell.

And if we do, thank God for His plans are perfect.
If we do not, thank God at least we met.

Ronella Hope Segaya, beWITCHed

Tell Me How It Feels

The sun of Punjab rises on your face and your perfume talks
about Faridkot.
7 months away from home, and deep in your heart you know
there is a lifetime more.
You swallow difficultly. You stop the tears say God can
always hear.
So you pray for strength, not to go running but you are near.
Tell me how it feels.

Your mom cries every time you call and it makes you not
wanting to call anymore.
Your dad is too old for his job but he never wants to quit.
Your brother is trying to reach out for help to save your house
being taking over.
Your niece is longing for your love and your lover.
Tell me how it feels.

My past keeps haunting you; your friends never let you sleep.
Never been in love but you confess for me, you fell too deep.
Tongue-tied on room 63, I cannot breathe.
I think there is nothing else that can make me leave.
Tell me how it feels.

Afraid of the consequences but you still break the rules.
You say time will heal all kind of wounds.
Let you cover me with affection and lust,
We pray together, "For a lifetime may God make this last,"
Tell me how it feels.

Now, the pandemic forbids us to do what we do,
The same city, different beds, we stay at home.
Every thought leads me thinking about you.
Tell me how it feels so I will know if you feel the same way as
I do.

Ronella Hope Segaya, beWITCHed

Stay

Stay and make this right or you can choose to suffocate me.
Respect an older night so you will be clever enough to see
Shake your head and say no, baby you do not have to be okay.
Hold my hands and keep me close. I will guard you on your
darkest days.

Keep your feet glued on the ground where we first met.
You will see me there when the sun rises and set.
I will make paradise exist for you if I have to.
Sirsari, Faridkot is not the only place for you.

Stay and brush my hair or you can choose to burn me alive.
The fog is thick and mountains are high enough but you
cannot hide.
My eyes are the secret passages to the soul of your lover.
Tangle your arms around me. I will make cold days hotter.

You are my home and let me be yours, my heart.
You never have to wonder at 2 am who loves you and who
does not.
Fill your cup, even make it overflow to show you who does.
Only then, maybe you will stay for one more day or a lifetime
more.

Stay.

Ronella Hope Segaya, beWITCHed

AT 20

College friends, perfect faces, imperfect lives.
Pray again. This time longer, recite it louder.
Spend the whole night on crowded streets,
Dancing and singing bare feet.
We kiss tongue-tied, at the corner near the stoplight.
The only witness is the moon that shines bright.
My Jesus is your God and the choir calls our name,
I'm happy, your hope and love, we bathe in the rain.
And I said, 54 hearts only yours is beating.
At twenty you're the air I'm breathing.
You are the best gift this world ever gave me,
If only you could talk and understand English good, but you
don't.
So I'll spend my whole life learning Punjabi
So I could put my feelings into words.
A year from now your friends will find out
About this little secret, we keep without a doubt.
Embrace myself because the suitcase of my past is still
underneath my bed.
And my box of mistakes is still hiding in my closet.
The pockets of my jeans have holes,
Put your hand inside and feel the fire in my core.
Because you light me up the way no one ever could,
And you hold my hand under the table like we should.
We hold hands because we should.
Like love should be free.
Like we should be allowed to love if it's meant to be.
However, I learned it in college that we don't always get what
we want.
So we are secretly meeting again in the dark.
Passing through the busy midnight street,
Face covered, high speed, like criminals, some kind of thieves.

Ronella Hope Segaya, beWITCHed

What Does Punjab Looks Like?

I do not smoke but my mouth tastes like cigarettes
Moreover, the color of my expired matt lipstick lingers on
your lips.
The room smells like the richness and royalty of Punjab
You are the best villager Faridkot could ever have.
Break the rules because you have been obeying them for 24
years.
I am confused but certain that I have never been this happy
for 20 years.
Snakebites and angels
Midnight drives and gold bells.
What does Punjab looks like?

All the colors under the blue sky,
All the rupees you keep inside your pocket
The cold morning gets through your jacket
Mini beds scatter on your dusty front yard,
The lovers secretly held hands late on the backyard.
I thought Romeo and Juliet only exist on Shakespeare's mind,
Love could draw anything but a straight line.
Sometimes, you fall in love without reason
Your body heat was never out of the season.
Castles in the mid of rice fields and dungeons,
We celebrate with roti and sabje one December afternoon.
It has always been a question of ...
What does Punjab looks like,

'Cause curiosity loves me more than I love myself.
Usually, these unusual faces set the sunrise to the west.
And makes me swallow my best friend's spit.
What does Punjab looks like?
I have never been there but I have heard it looks like here.
If you argue then take me there.

Ronella Hope Segaya, beWITCHed

However, boy, you do not have to fly me; do not need a
connecting flight in Singapore
Take me to a rendezvous. A nice room will do.
Let me stare at your brown eyes and let me say Punjab looks
like you.

Ronella Hope Segaya, beWITCHed

When You Are in Love

When you love, there is more than just a mouthful of pain. You go crazy down the streets, wide-awake all night. You have to eat whatever kind of taste it may bring to your tongue whether sweet or bitter or a combination of both tears and laugh.

When you love, it makes photographs in your nightstand. You look into it deep; see a million reasons to smile but you hear the thunderstorms knocking in your windowpane. It breaks your heart with a crumpled paper in your hand.

'Cause when you are in love, you are addicted to that scent that you smell in the bed sheets and you never want to let it go. Please never let it go because when you open up the door and let her in, you know you have everything that you need. She is all you need.

'Cause when you are in love you're taking photographs of every moment even though you feel like crying. I know you are crying. 'Cause when you hug her from her back, you feel the needles in your chest. Her back is in your chest.

'Cause you are in love, you get to go through everything. When you feel it, it simply gets easier, and then gets complicated. You involve yourself into something bigger than the galaxies in the universe. When you try to figure it, you are solving an equation without a correct answer. You can spend your whole life stuck in a room without a door but you will never know what it means, what it want to say or what it knows. Only when you give up

Ronella Hope Segaya, beWITCHed

'Cause when you are in love you know there is no going back. You have to cry, you have to laugh, but you never want to go. Never let her go. 'Cause when the sun starts to rise, you know you will be seeing her again and you try to kiss her passionately. Kiss her slowly.

'Cause when you are in love your mind runs a thousand miles out of the country and you just fly there through the wind, and when you close the curtains in the bedroom to hide the sunset, you know she is sleeping in your arms again. You will be making love again.

He is in love. She is in love. They are in love but they still cry without telling each other. However, they are trying to be better because they are better.

Ronella Hope Segaya, beWITCHed

Something So Real

I have been searching the city for a love that would stay.
Darling you searched three countries, daily you prayed.
The sun wished to meet the moon but never would.
I traced your footsteps and found you up on the woods.
Boy, I found you underneath the stars.
Deep inside your shirt, there were shining scars.
Silver and gold, your eyes looked up to mine.
I decided to stop searching and planted you on my mind.
Something so real not just something to feel

You said we were not kids anymore.
You brought me home and opened the door.
The pieces of your heart were scattered on the floor.
You said you never felt so sure before.
Suddenly you did when our eyes met.
You wiped my tears and the curtains were wet.
You said you wondered how to dance in a storm,
Held my hand to your chest and it started to roam
Something so real not just something to feel

Baby we started flying late one night.
Never wanted to let go, never wanted to fight.
Stopped by your friend to say hello and goodbye
We let the midnight burn out our own lies.
Dreaming of rings, parties, and everything in between
We signed an imaginary contract never to sin.
We kissed and danced, vanished on your father's land.
We cleaned our feet and dusted off the sand.
Something so real not just something to feel

I would walk mountains, fires and oceans with you.
I bet you would save your last breath for me, too.
Thank you for loving me, thank you for staying.

Ronella Hope Segaya, beWITCHed

Thank you for not getting tired of praying.
We stood there underneath the stars.
I watched the moon light erased your scars.
For a million times, I would say still.
What we have is something so real not just something to feel.

Ronella Hope Segaya, beWITCHed

Waiting Down Here

He is home from the famous galaxy.
His face is moist and he smells like twenty-three.
He does not remember what day is today.
I wonder if time exists in Milky Way.

Scars from his back are from the shooting stars.
He tried to avoid the meteors coming to get it far.
He buzzes when he talks and backward he walks.
He forgets to bring money when he shops.

He misses the moon and looks for the sun.
He says rain is so much fun.
He looks at me as if I am a shining Venus.
I cannot do anything, cannot even focus.

He tells me he almost fell for Mercury.
He was flying through the spaces he says he missed me.
I ask him what does Saturn looks like.
He said he counted a hundred and fifty-three satellites.

So I say,
Tell me, did the meteorites help you cleared your mind?
Is there anything the scientists yet to find?
Did you wonder what does a bigger universe looks like?
Tell me, when is your next flight?
It does not matter you know I will still be waiting down here,
Under your mother's cheap chandelier
Come back after three years,
I promise I will never be wasting tears.
The only thing I will ask from you is,

Ronella Hope Segaya, beWITCHed

Babe when the colors seem too bright, I want you to
think of me.

He packs again for his trip to the constellations.
I convince myself he is just leaving for vacation.
I do not want to stop him or else he will think I am not
happy when he sees the earth from afar,
He says I am his life's biggest star.

On the 28th, I am hoping he will remember his way back
to me.
I bet his smell will be like twenty-six.
I will tie myself under his mother's chandelier.
Keep my heart in a box for three years.

Ronella Hope Segaya, beWITCHed

You breathed me in like oxygen
That sustained your lungs.
Not too long, you breathed me out
Of your life like carbon dioxide

Ronella Hope Segaya, beWITCHed

The Pain

I looked closer to the blurry halo that sits outside your brain but I overlooked your demons painting blood in your face.

Bewitched by your poisonous love overflowing from my cup,

The pain was clogging in my system, causing my breathing to stop.

Ronella Hope Segaya, beWITCHed

You never came back.

I gave myself out to you
*as **a home** just for you*
*to treat me like a **vacation house***

Ronella Hope Segaya, beWITCHed

You were not the man I loved.
You were the poem I wrote.
You were the sunset that ended my day.
You were the knife stabbed in my heart.

Ronella Hope Segaya, beWITCHed

*And sometimes I ask myself,
is he worth the fight?*

Ronella Hope Segaya, beWITCHed

I watched myself forgave you
 again and again until there
was no space for forgiveness
to myself on how much I trusted
you after all the lies I'd let you tell me.

Ronella Hope Segaya, beWITCHed

No one knows the
intentions *of love,*
*not unless it **breaks** your heart.*

Ronella Hope Segaya, beWITCHed

Every time I feel my heart crashes, you will call and I will keep giving chances. I keep forgiving you as much as I keep forgiving myself for loving you.

Ronella Hope Segaya, beWITCHed

I *sipped in* the last drop of your favorite black coffee as I watched you **bombard** my phone with calls you know I would never pick. The right side of my head told me to at least make things clear to you but the left side, with the higher volume screamed," **leave the box before it's too late**,".

Ronella Hope Segaya, beWITCHed

It all started on that street.
Few weeks passed and it ended on the very exact
corner.

Ronella Hope Segaya, beWITCHed

Is the spark gone?
Or am I making things up in my head?

Ronella Hope Segaya, beWITCHed

Would I ever cross your mind?
Would you ever go back to the nights we had fights
on turning on and off the lights?
Would you eat ice cream again?
Would you keep the promises made when you
cuddled me on the bed and said, "You're my best
friend"?

Ronella Hope Segaya, beWITCHed

In a very certain time of my life now,
I find myself constantly searching for freedom.

Ronella Hope Segaya, beWITCHed

I tried. I tried so fucking hard to tell you it was not me.
 It was my broken soul asking for a little time.
My fucking art makes me want to feel the pain.
It was my lustful desire to go out with men of ships, of planes, of the fields. I know these things because men tried it upon me, begged me to be their taste test.
I found it addicting but it was
not me who shattered you to pieces.
It was my actions.
I wanted to stop.
 I tried so fucking hard but
end up doing the same mistakes.
Call me evil but it was not me
that tore you apart.
 It was you.
 It was your love for me.
 It was your trust.
 It was your stupidity.

Ronella Hope Segaya, beWITCHed

And maybe...
Just maybe...
You will be happy to see me leave

Ronella Hope Segaya, beWITCHed

In the spaces between my fingers, I can see the emptiness of my soul and I can't help but feel like I belong somewhere else and the strangers are better companions than the people I surround myself with. It's not anxiety. It's neither depression nor desperation. It's loneliness. It's the hunger for a love that I can't seem to get a hold of, a love that doesn't exist in my environment. I can't help but feel like I only breathe to exist but not to be alive.

Ronella Hope Segaya, beWITCHed

*Where do you go when you're
not lost but do not belong to a place?*

Ronella Hope Segaya, beWITCHed

No lovers allowed
Only strangers

Hotel Room 63

Burn me to ashes, my beloved for I, myself is submitting to infidelity and there's no way of denying that my inside is screaming, wanting to go walk the midnight streets.
Such a splendid mistake and I'll do it over and over again if given the chance because I'm addicted to the smell of the foreign sheets.

This is honesty to me, telling you of the darkness in my seemed too bright face and character when my mother's around me.
Be wise enough to listen in my plea and pack immediately my stuffs in your house. Send them back to the place where you first met me.

Ronella Hope Segaya, beWITCHed

I loved you and it was probably the best lie I have managed to keep underneath my tongue for four fucking years. I told you with legs wide open. I told you with my unzipped dress. I told you with my scars plastered on my skin but you overlooked the truth. You did not know what honesty looks like. You did not know what does shit sounds like.

You thought the world owed you for cleaning a woman like me. You thought you were enough to change me. It never occurred to you that there are stains you can't just wash off. There are people you can't just change. Blame me all you want but your foolishness doesn't give you justice.

Ronella Hope Segaya, beWITCHed

Words Out

You were dancing in your hotel room with the shirt we
bought downtown;
You never missed a line that I wrote in my poetry
collection;
Or at least that was what you said before the fall out,
you were a clown;
Wishing someone could have warned me of the sand
storm and your intentions.
All I ever gave you was honesty, so stupid to believe that
you would give it back,
Tried involving myself to a hurricane that you made, my
beloved
But all you ever made me see was your shits in the lies
and your fucks,
I had let you complete me but the transparency wasn't
enough.
For you I was just another toy, bought and enjoyed,
useless figure
Swore to the stars never let anyone inside again, fought
the pain
To me, love became a funny thing; I was laughing but
not so sure.
Left before I go insane but you clutched my brain, wary
of the planes.

Supposed to be free now but you're all I could think of
to write about
So I wonder back to the days you still had me there, let
the words out

Ronella Hope Segaya, beWITCHed

64th Post

Pronounce the words as if you own the world.
Hypocrites surround you.
Graceless powers in your hands but you do not
understand why they left you.
Maybe it was something you said; maybe it was
something you did.
Controllable storms at the back of your head.
Convenient traffic was parading your streets.
You could not stop shaking. Your brain was over
thinking.
Restlessness forbade you from breathing.

You lost all sense chasing the sun.
Crossing your fingers praying you were the one.
Kneeled on the 64th post asked," Why I cannot be
enough,
To people that claims love is enough."

Settle at a foreign land and be a stranger, no more.
No one really called your whole name before.
Your lungs and your systems cannot sustain their needs.
You are but a stopover with field of unlucky seeds.
They kiss you, and own you for bitter nights they feel
unsure.
Take your gold then leave you in the cold and dirty floor.

You lost all sense walking in the rain.
Alone in the dark you enjoyed the pain.
Broken on the 64th post asked," Why I cannot be
enough,
To people that claims love is enough."

Ronella Hope Segaya, beWITCHed

Sidewalks

I smell you in the wet pavements on sidewalks where we used to stroll at nights.
There is an inevitable sting of pain throbbing in my chest and I know why.
What I have now are memories to remember underneath the shameless stars.
Looking back, love was rude and life took you so far.

For a while, you felt like home to my veins and me.
You were the calming wind on my busy midnight streets.
You stabbed my heart and I stole your shirt hanging on your friend's wall.
You bet I still wear it at times I feel lonely and cold.

Somehow, I felt like I was worth the space in the world.
Although not for long, you crashed my self-made value.
I still have nightmares of you in the hour of darkness in my room.
You came to my life in a fast-motion and left too soon.

Pictures of us in your couch are still raw in my mind.
You said you would always be in love at the back of your hand.
You pulled a string of hair in my head and tied it to your finger like a ring.
I was not sure what it meant back then.

Breakable, naive and, young I was when you took advantage of me.

Ronella Hope Segaya, beWITCHed

I had let you harassed my peace of mind and I had let
you win.
The flames of this cruel and inhumane heartbreak
burned my skin.

Out of sight, you flew away from the mess your sweet
words made.
I tell you now, no amount of years can make this ache
fade.
You must have not cared at all when you packed your
things away.
I saw you all over with someone else as I was strolling
back on that sidewalk yesterday.

Ronella Hope Segaya, beWITCHed

Mercy

Long streets, they never understood what was between
you and me.
Car rides; we went to places and pretended to be the
royals we could never be.
Strange fights, in spiral motion we were running out of
words to say.
Blurred lights, the heartbreak looked clearer than the
road we took that day.

With shaky voice, I said I could not take the heat
anymore.
With hesitation, you said you never felt so cold before.
With wounded chest, I slammed the car door and
walked my way home alone.
With disappointed face, you picked and burned all my
scratches deep down your bones.

Sometimes it ends when both hearts know the feelings
are not enough.
Sometimes it breaks when two souls fail to find the real
love.
Sometimes it hurts when the person you love the most is
too ready to let go.
Sometimes it stings when it kills you but you cannot
show.

Haunting ghosts, we were on our favorite spot in town.
Colorless fireworks, it kept my feet glued on the ground.
Sleepless hours, your scream, to me was a familiar sound.
Timeless years, wished I could soften a smile that you
stoned.

Ronella Hope Segaya, beWITCHed

With hopeless tears, I stood there at my doorstep
wondering where you have been.
With careless thoughts, I knew you were never coming
back again.
With ripe red wine, I drank all the pains and memories
down my belly.
Buried albums of reminiscence and throw a sober party.

Sometimes it is strange when you realize you do not
need anyone to breathe.
Sometimes it has to ripen first before you could even use
the seed.
Sometimes it does not seem like a mercy when someone
breaks your heart.
Sometimes it has to end first before you can restlessly
start.

Ronella Hope Segaya, beWITCHed

Ghost Letter

I want to convince myself that you stay up late at night,
See through everything even with no lights,
I want you to miss the silent conversations turn to fights,
Never go to sleep unless things are right

I want you to look out on the streets, search for traces of me,
Wonder on places we have been at three.

I bet you keep your phone right now next to you
Glue your eyes on the screen as I used to.
Babe, it takes every little thing on me not to call you
I bet you are also going insane thinking what to do.

I want you to crowd your mind with the possibility that I am
getting over you,
Question your dying cells how you missed the due
I want you to make love to me under the moon inside your
mind,
Clear out highways and check my lifeline

I want you to go and take the final step back at my door
With white roses and candles to throw at my bedroom floor

I bet you blame yourself for letting me drive your Rover,
That night was so fast and all I knew was I was your lover.
Today, as they walk me back to where I came from,
You are nowhere and out of sight under the happy sun.

Ronella Hope Segaya, beWITCHed

Where Is Home?

Have you ever wondrously walked in the midnight streets?
Under the blanket full of diamonds sparkling in colors
The city was at rest, leaving danger to the late goers.

Tucked myself, afraid but did it anyway.
When you are not like most girls, what difference does it
make?
Let go of my biggest dreams and promises.

Where to go when you are not lost but do not belong to a
place?
12:39 and the world seemed asleep but I was sitting on
esplanade bench.
Thinking, "What went wrong, who to blame, or which way to
go,"

Caught a teardrop on my left hand,
Wiped it and decided to go home,
Ah, I remembered I did not have a home.

Ronella Hope Segaya, beWITCHed

Daisies Between Her Legs

He kept watering the flowers between her thighs and she had
let him picked up fresh daisies.
After a romantic night and a feast-like dinner, he went out of
his way and left nothing but dirty dishes.
He visited her every now and then.
She always welcomed him with legs wide open.

I let him took advantage of her.

He said he did not belong to someone else but he never came
home at night.
She tried so hard not to cry during their first fight on her first
flight to the Milky Way.
He never walked out in the dark, afraid his mistakes might
keep up. He stayed in the fire light,
And she held the torch behind his back, followed him to
another woman's house all the way.

I blew the fire and watched her cry.

He promised her the world without a ring to put on her finger
but she thought it was okay.
She knew she was not the only one but she never dared
speaking up for herself.
He smiled as he waved another goodbye and paved his way to
another vacation house,
She was not so sure which tourist spot he headed next so she
waited patiently.

I let him destroyed her.

The next morning, I woke on the same bed and body,

Ronella Hope Segaya, beWITCHed

For the first time in my life, I bravely pulled the blooming flowers out between my thighs and left the weeds.
When he came back the next few days, he saw the dying daisies on my doorstep.
He asked himself if he really forgot to water them before he left.

I let myself went to rest.

Would Never Love Again

From a small yet famous town,
Just three hamlets away from the city,
There was a woman whose brain was crowded by thoughts of you.

When nine of the night came,
She stared at the moon just above her and you,
Wishing you were wondering about her, too.

If not her, who would be wasting tears for you?
If not you, whom would she be writing her love letters to?

She was too full from the silence of the night,
So she cried to hear her sobs and turned out the lights,
Praying God would listen to her heart.

When morning came, it was still you,
What pill could she buy to minimize your presence on her mind?
She checked her phone but still no traces of you.

It was her instinct to get dressed and travel the distance,
To at least say hi and goodbye for the last time
No amount of sound could hide the loud beating in her chest.

She again found herself on your doorstep.
Was about to knock when she heard someone singing,
But it wasn't your voice that entered her ears uninvited.

It was not unfamiliar. She knew that woman's voice very well.
Twelve years growing up, and she did not know what to feel.
She could not figure out what her best friend was doing on your house.

Ronella Hope Segaya, beWITCHed

So she left, never looked back.
Swore to the stars, she would never love again.

There you were on your apartment pacing back and forth,
To call her or not to call, did not know what you were
waiting for,
You ended up throwing yourself on the couch where she used
to sleep.

You looked out to the city; the moon was shining bright,
You were wondering if she was even thinking about you.
Next to your heart was your phone waiting for traces of her.

If not you, who would keep the memories you made with her?
If not her, whom would you be singing your songs to?

You did not want to admit but the tears could not hide no
more.
Your arms missed twisting around her. She was all you could
think of.
You let the lights blind you that night.

When the sun was out, you knew it was a new morning,
You woke up without her next to you.
You thought of overdosing and suicide.

Your brother called, said he was on his way with her
girlfriend,
Your brother must be lucky to have her best friend.
With little hope, you got dressed and wrote a note "I am
getting her back, bro,"

You found yourself on the bus, an hour later you were on her
town.
Rushed through her house, rang the doorbell for 28th time

Ronella Hope Segaya, beWITCHed

However, she was not home.

It was too late, you thought.
Looking back to the days she said, forever you and her
But that was long gone. You went back home.

With dead dreams, you opened your door
Her best friend and your brother were singing on the living room,
With fake smile, you locked yourself on your room.

Promised God, you would never go back to that town again.
Promised God, you would never love again.

She moved on, so did you.

Ronella Hope Segaya, beWITCHed

Eleventh Street

You knew I have been patrolling the town with a
Fortuner I could not afford.
I was a little sadist so I enjoyed watching everybody
when I was bored.
Then you met me on the eleventh street, one block
before my sight has died,
I loved the visions in my head when they started
switching on the city's light.

You knew I needed some time when you asked for my
name so you could label me.
Tried to reach the stars to breathe but could not even
stand on a tree.
Scanned the horizon of this earth's possibilities with
mind full of red and gold,
What do you do when your soul, the only thing you own
was sold?

You knew I was good at messing things up but you did
not stop.
Picked up the lilies at your neighbor's backyard, tied it
and wrapped.
I watched you paint my sky with pastel white, safron
and green.
Those colors saved India and pushed *her* to win.

You knew I was falling so you kept the doubts at the
back of your mind.
The question of whether you should or should not.

Ronella Hope Segaya, beWITCHed

Kissed the edged of my lips and you smelt like freedom
and victory,
So I held on tight to your shirt and became the woman
you said I should be.

You knew you became the air that sustained my lungs.
You were the blood that crowded my veins and the pail
to my sand.
The mornings seemed brighter with the sun coming
from the west,
I was on a new behavior doing my best.

You knew your footsteps away from me would tear my
heart.
All the words and shiny jewelries looked genuine at the
start.
I neither saw the storm coming nor heard the thunder.
You packed up your things and walked out from the
door of your lover.

You knew I ran around breaking in the houses I could
not afford.
Showed up on parties uninvited when I was bored.
I heard your whispers on the wind, only that it was too
slow.
You left the lilies at the eleventh street to grow.

Went back to the eleventh street,
Six months gone and you still haunt my brain.
In the middle of fast cars, I walked on the green light
Somehow hoping you would come back one more night.

Ronella Hope Segaya, beWITCHed

Should I

Should I feel proud?
I was the one you left her for,
Could not see the reason, could not figure out
I was there wasted and confused on the floor.
You left without telling her why.
She was a year older than I was.
Broke her without saying goodbye,
Left her on slow motion while you were on rush.

Should I feel happy?
Man, you brighten up my world but she was alone.
As you took her torch out from her way,
You switched on all the lights in my room.
I found out early yesterday morning.
About her tears with a broken heart,
I was on bliss while she was mourning.
To keep us close, I made it too far.

Should I feel lucky?
You built my house as you destroyed hers.
What did you do when you were lonely, baby?
I found this love like a curse.
People always say past is past.
You promised me you would make this last,
The fears were dancing in my head.
You left her too easy, Am I next?

Ronella Hope Segaya, beWITCHed

Our Young and Old Nights

I knew the closet was half-empty.
I knew I could not stop that day to come.
Have you had enough and grew bored of me?
I was shameless and my heart was numb.

I knew it when you dropped the glasses on the kitchen
floor,
I knew it when you slammed the door.
My guts told me when you said you were not so sure,
If you really have been in love before

The night was young but you were running wild
Again, I had to breathe it out and reconcile.
You were itching and could not wait to be free
You were burning just as you wanted to be
Broke the windows because you knew you could.
Jumped out and disappeared into the woods.

I wondered sometimes late at night,
Have you ever missed the screaming and fights?
Hoping you would appear on our doorstep one day,
Would ask for forgiveness," sorry," you say

I knew you were too far when I called out your name
I knew it when the sheets were folded the same
My hands sent out sixty-eight letters
Should I wait for nothing forever?

The night was old but you were still not home.
Again, I had to close the curtains and sleep all alone.
Thirteen months ago, you ran and went free

Ronella Hope Segaya, beWITCHed

Was the fire still burning? You were too far to see.

I never fixed the windows that you broke.
Just as you left and scattered the pieces of my soul.
And if you haven't really been in love before,
Give my heart back and light the candles at four
This, my only request before you leave again,
Remember my face when you broke the glasses on the kitchen.

Ronella Hope Segaya, beWITCHed

School Friends

Sometimes I wonder at cold nights,
When the silence seems over occurring,
I let the flicker of the yellow light,
Bring back scenes in my brain.

Do they still remember the days we ruled our own little
kingdom beside the church?
The teachers said we were the best batch but also the worse.
Stolen answers, forgotten home works, and many on the spot
plays,
They tried taking the crown but we were enjoying the
glorious days.

Worn-out friendships, tiptoed leaderships, they envied the
palace,
We were praying to grow up fast but never thought things
would last.
We laughed and we cried, joy, obedience, charity and love.
At the fifth year, I ran away with a phrase I had enough.

We fell down out of fake smiles and backstabbing memories.
They never let me rest and never let me sleep.
I knew the words even I was far away.
I knew they would have never cared even if I stayed.

At the heart of the city, I found a bigger world.
New faces and chances I was out of words.
We met on the second floor but it was never a better place.
I was at the top with tear-dropping case.

I had five royalties who walked with me.
On canteen, accounting, library even on foreign streets,
We finished the end but it also meant,
That we finished everything in between

Ronella Hope Segaya, beWITCHed

College was the shortest but the best months of my life.
Respect, forgiveness, friendships, I felt alive.
They still laugh at my dreams and I still go to places with them.
I still know what they look like and hear the sounds of them.

I thank you for making me, who I am now.
With fifteen years of spending my life at school,
I realize at twenty, we do not get to remember every lesson in biology and history in life.
However, we keep those people, good and bad forever at the back of our minds.

Ronella Hope Segaya, beWITCHed

Where Are You Now, Babe?

That night is still clear in my memory.
The lights were out but I saw you at 12:53
You brushed strains of hair out of my face.
You said you were in love and that you would never change.
Where are you now, babe?

As I write this file down, I keep asking my brain,
What went wrong and who was to blame?
That August 28, when you took the plane,
What pushed you to go so far away?
Where are you now, babe?

As I sit on my window looking out at the street,
I always kind of weeping when I hear that beat,
Your smell is still on the shirt you left on my floor.
I never imagined you walking out of my door.
Where are you now, babe?

I wonder if you still have pictures of me.
As I touch yours and keep them in my bed beneath.
I know it was eight months ago and time gone by so fast.
You must have known things between us would last.
Where are you now, babe?

I still remember when you were taking your steps.
I tried keeping but I lost my breaths.
It is 24th of April now and someone is making me laugh.
I wonder why for you I was not enough.
Where are you now, babe?

As I think of words to rhyme up the lines,
I wish someone had nudged me to look on the signs.
We were nothing but poems to end.
As I end this, with someone else I shall begin.

Ronella Hope Segaya, beWITCHed

Where are you now babe?

I watch the stars in the sky fade like the scenes in your
favorite movie.
I bet you do not even remember my name because I was
nothing but a fantasy.
I avoid running into your friends around the city.
I try not to ask again today.
Where are you now, babe?

Ronella Hope Segaya, beWITCHed

I Swear Boy

There we were at two in the morning.
We were shifting sides laughing about my ripped jeans size.
I watched you and me smiled as the YouTube do the talking.
I was sure I was right but I was certain you were wise.
I swore, boy everything was all right.

There we were in the bathroom floor.
Playing jackstone and filling our throats with coke.
Cried for a dozen movies, only stopped when our eyes were sore
Prayed for a lifetime more, bodies were shaking and soaked.
I swore, boy everything was all right.

There we were at eight in the morning.
You sipped my coffee and gave me your warmest kiss.
We danced around the kitchen singing.
My dad kept calling and I missed.
I swore, boy everything was all right.

There we were at the bedroom window.
I was screaming who was calling you at midnight.
That was why I never wanted to say hello.
I knew at the back of my mind, it was just another goodbye.
I swore, boy everything was all right.

There we were one in the afternoon.
You were pacing back and forth did not know what to say.
I was thinking the storm was coming soon.
You did not notice the rain that day.
I swore, boy everything was all right.

There we were outside on the first corner of your mother's street.
We were fighting and going insane about our fate.

Ronella Hope Segaya, beWITCHed

The world decided first before we could even let our eyes
meet.
I loved my life but my heart was full of hate.
I swore, boy everything was all right.

There we were at ten in the evening.
I locked the gate so you could not get in.
We fell out of interest to continue loving.
We stumbled on our feet trying not to drop our sins.
I swore, boy everything was all right.

Here I am again at two in the morning.
I am somewhat nostalgic with the weather and everything.
We used to watch the moon around this time.
Here you are running in my mind.
I swear, boy this time I will be fine.

Ronella Hope Segaya, beWITCHed

This Love

Pull me closer to your chest,
I want to hear your beating heart.
With me, you do not have to be the best,
I will never let them draw us apart.
We are dancing in your room.
The gravity is not touching my feet.
Late one night you walk me back home,
There is magic sparkling around the street.

I can see this alley is dark and dangerous,
I can hear my heartbeat getting precarious,
I can smell you and your smoke in my bed,
I can feel this love is about to mess my head,
So I get ready for it.

I can picture out your face,
Like a scar at the back of my hand.
We are falling out of grace.
Stay in our place and sleep on foreign land.
We are similar on taste we argue all the time.
We secretly live with our mistakes,
Fake a smile and pretend that we are fine.
Too scared to admit it is too late.

I can see this path is chaotic and risky,
I can hear you sobbing after a glass of whiskey,
I can smell your poison brushed on the plates,
I can feel this love running out of time to wait,
So I write down our fate.

We are both afraid to admit we are halfway alive.
The mess is covering your tiled bedroom floor.
We cannot make this love survive.

Ronella Hope Segaya, beWITCHed

We do not dance on your bedroom anymore.
With a bag full of tears and stolen clothes,
I am walking home alone.
I make myself believe I am a ghost.
However, the magic around the street is gone.

I can see you from here.
I can hear you everywhere.
I can smell you all the time.
I can feel this love is a sign.
So I let another meteor pass me by.

Ronella Hope Segaya, beWITCHed

Someone New

I strolled by the sidewalk late November,
I was searching for someone new.
The last time I wrote a poem was last summer.
Now, I have to find another view.
I was looking up at the stars and moon.
Praying someone would appear soon.

I met Harpreet on the 28th, two months after my birthday.
He called me late, escaped daddy I was twenty with many
things to say.
I cannot remember what exactly his first words were that
night.
However, I could tell in detail what happened to us under the
blurry light.

I went home the next morning with overflowing brain.
I memorized him as I ran on the pouring rain.
On my neighbor's parking lot, I started the poem in my head.
I entered my door, dried myself and finished the first verse on
my bed.

The roses in your head are beautiful like your Punjab.
In the black matter of my brain, I know it is love.
Poisoned with past threads laced over my heart,
My veins are unsure where to start.
You make me believe in fairytales again.
For so long I cannot remember when.
This time, I will try my best not to see the end.
Make you stay and give you friends.

I remembered his brown eyes melting me like an ice cream.
He made me worried about their words like an uninvited
scream.
He promised me impossible things and a ring.

Ronella Hope Segaya, beWITCHed

We ended up on the 68th corner fighting.

I went home that night with tears on my cheeks.
I tried to stay but also tried to drag my feet.
The night was cold but his voice was colder.
The second verse was made near my mother's locker.

Funny it is to think that we would last.
The happy nights and blinding days went by so fast.
As I write this second and last verse,
I am kind of thinking that love is a cruel curse.
It was all rainbows and butterflies at first.
At the end, we both went mad of thirst.
I am ending this with a line so real and delicate.
Perhaps, to love again someone new is never too late.

I strolled by the sidewalk late December,
I was searching for someone new.
The last time I wrote a poem was last late November.
Now, I have to find another view.
I was looking up at the stars and moon.
Praying someone would appear soon.

Someone did.

Ronella Hope Segaya, beWITCHed

Grin

How much it cost her to drop everything and let go.
Darling, we both knew that we did not know.
She dressed like summer out in a cold weather blow.
Broken inside and dying but she did not need to show.

How much time she had before she knew there was a falling
out?
Darling, we both knew what this was all about.
She was a freezing coffee but a brand new cup of tea.
There were a whole lot of hidden tattoos we never had to see.

I saw her this morning as she drove pass my street.
Darling, we both knew whom she was going to meet.
She wore that treacherous cat smile she wears when she is off
to something.
I bet tonight: she is going home blaming the stars for shining.

Tom used to tel her,"You smell so sweet, honey"
Darling, we both knew he never liked candies.
Rebekah replied with the widest grin this whole town has
ever seen.
She went in his father's car and let him drove to places she
had never been.

Too young to let the whole world fool you.
Not all those shooting stars make dreams come true.
My friend Rebekah would you listen if I tell you?
Men like Tom, they go run around and trick you.

So soon you will get well, will get rid of a sick love song dear.
Stuck your car with cases of red horse beer
Rebekah darling the whole city knew this time would come.
So we wait here in my window, I know you will pass my
street at one.

Ronella Hope Segaya, beWITCHed

How did she end up dead voice and comatose?
Darling, we both fail to know how thing goes.
Tom led the party with announcement and wine toast.
She looked out to the midnight avenue once before she
overdosed.

How did she escape love in its cruelest face?
Darling, we both fail to check her in the remaining days.
Rude rules she kept under her skirt and thought she found
the one.
It was fine getting rid of him but now she is the one that is
gone.

I saw her at the back of my head and she never left.
Darling, we both fail to appear on her doorstep.
I could smell her on the eight am breeze as I opened up my
windowpane.
I bet tonight: she never had to go through pain again.

I heard Tom told her, "You smell so sweet, honey"
Darling, we both knew he never liked candies.
Vickie replied with the widest grin and the town took it as a
sign.
The whispers came they said, "Tom will do it again this time,"

Ronella Hope Segaya, beWITCHed

Leaving Soon

Tell me I am all you wanted before I start expiring for you,
lips turning blue.
Take me to the street where I first met your mom and sister,
to the very near corner, my feet: I glued.
Show me my love, every flaw hidden at the back of your mind;
assure me your lies,
I am leaving soon.

If you have something to say,
Tomorrow is too late.
I am leaving soon.

The rooftop thrill feels so good now.
I can see the stores we shopped in downtown.
This might be the last time I am seeing them out,
I am leaving soon.
Empty conversations on a fully charged phone
Tonight, I am never going to make it home,
Standing face to face with the moon alone,
I am leaving soon.

Have you seen my fair-weathered friends?
Sour faces and their vibrant colored judgments
Tell them, I am sick of crying
I am leaving soon.

Ronella Hope Segaya, beWITCHed

Don't Blame Me

Don't blame me. It was the love that made me stripped my dress and appeared defenseless before those clowns I took home while my roommate's sleeping in the couch cuddled with someone she just met too. It was the love that made me forget every single word to schizophrenia's definition a minute before my final exam started. It was the love that made me search on streets for the idea of everything not just of something.

Don't blame me it was the same love that made me cut all threads connecting me to my best friends of sixteen years. The same love that made me swallow my foes' spit in search for a better stand in an argument. The same love that made me lose it at the debate of whether to or not to allow marijuana at school.

Don't blame me it was the same love that made me detached myself from the poisonous society. The same love that jailed me inside my own visions and endless hope of being able to catch the right star. The same love that made me want to take the hills instead of highways driving with my ambitions and stupidity.

Don't blame me. It was the love that made me write every single poem my father refuses to read every time I pile it up to his desks. It was love that made me ask for time like alms that is worth begging for. It was love that made me a poet unbothered with the revelations of my own words and how other people take them.

Ronella Hope Segaya, beWITCHed

Don't blame me. It was the same love that made me finish the compilation I hid under my sheets, scared my mother would find out what I did those times I wasn't home. It was the same love that made me keep coming back for more like a stone addict far from salvation. It was the same love that broke me into pieces.

Don't blame me. It was the same love that made me an awkward idiot whenever in a conversation with someone I like. It was the same love that made me changed my name to every single part of the world. It was the same love that took my face, erased it and put up someone I could not even recognize.

Don't blame me. It wasn't my intention to be like this; to be tasteless and boring. It was the past love that molded me into this woman I could never be proud of.

Ronella Hope Segaya, beWITCHed

The Revenge: Revival

Bewitched by the smell of freedom

Ronella Hope Segaya, beWITCHed

You are not worthy
of every step I
take in the darkness.

Love is

I think love is the very first particle
of oxygen that touched my lungs

The right to live
The freedom to breathe
The life itself is love to me

Ronella Hope Segaya, beWITCHed

Alive

Boycott the year; misread the road signs
Curse out your town for ninety-nine times
The traffic lights tell you to stop or go
I thought the sirens would save me it did not though
Write down the street where we first met

Dry out the pavements once you finished crying
Flood droughts the hearts of those tired of trying
Let go of the gut-wrenching pictures in your head
The one-sided love will never fill in the space in your bed
Close your eyes and project me at the dying sunset

Nothing but silence, what gives you peace and clarity
When you are sick in the restless and crowded city
Balancing the justice system inside my bedroom
With the suspect and the victim in one body alone
give but never forget to take what you can get

On my fresh years, no one told me of the bigger world
Dangerous and haunting, arranging my words
Familiar with the hide and seek we play in the woods
Picking freckles and damaging goods
Losing in car races and card bets

Tonight, the stars realign into something that looks like
your face
Ber-month saints in isolation days
Wrong assumptions and worst intentions
The path ahead is rainy but the distance travelled is the
validation
We come up with the solution that is death

Ronella Hope Segaya, beWITCHed

My friend, fate is neither truth nor lie
What you get are the fruits of what you plant in life
Stones that break and dismantle you into thin air
Stones that fix you as you grow your hair
You are not under six-feet yet

Ronella Hope Segaya, beWITCHed

Let Go of the Hound

Say goodbye to the dog you once took the bullet for
It's barking at you non-stop for letting a passerby
continue the journey
The reflections of yourself in your newly bought mirror
are not the reflections you are seeing now
Instead, it makes you believe that your hands are
covered with blood just because you opened the gates to
peace

Let go of the hound before it's too late, before it sinks its
teeth to your bones
For it made you felt like you're a perfect place but
darling, tell yourself you're a home
To the truth, to the justice, to the peace, to humanity, to
love and to freedom
Cut the dusty ribbons wrapped around your feet and
start drawing distance away from the masters of lambs

The bitch can't speak for herself, how can she speak for
poetry?
For what you are is what you write and what you write
is not limited to be labeled as what you want to be
But as what you want the world to be: rational, wide-
awake focused and kind
For every free country comes from a historical war in
constant rewind

Say goodbye. You have tried to be in control.
Let go when the pieces you're trying to build can't make
you whole.

Ronella Hope Segaya, beWITCHed

The Art of Leaving

You can always suffocate my thin arteries with your
naked lies;
Walk on eggshells whenever she ramps into my stormy-
themed parade,
Label me a bitch every time I stuff your bravado with my
decries,
Deny no more, the truth underneath your sin melted the
past decade
Wish me luck at the waiting verge of death, my sugar
coated mistake;
With violence, as the fast-changing skies for thunderous
miracle,
Less prayed but if ever, I will give you golden pass to my
dark wake;
Mourn or rejoice, you can but my frontline reason is
satirical
Keep me closer now that you still get a hold of my neck
in your palm,
Try not to loosen the grip, ultimate power over my
breathing,
Double check the memories at the back of your head,
stop not becalm
This is your last chance of wearing gold clothes. Treason
is coming, darling.

A woman can only stay for too much, not for the least
you can give,
She lives to perfect the art of leaving when she forgets
to forgive.

Ronella Hope Segaya, beWITCHed

Revival

Seems he does not take the damn time to read my
fucking poems anymore,
Pretend he does not see the endless ribbons wrapped
around my body,

Sure, there were summers but there were winters; it
wasn't that cold before,
Recognized my vision in the midnight sea: somebody
holding me

Baby, I tried so hard, surrendered every pieces of me to
you,
Wishing you would appear on my doorstep, back to my
violet skies,

But you chose to parade her streets, cut me out and
painted my heart blue
Is it just me? Darling, my brain keeps chasing for the
unanswered whys

Savoring the sweetness of my heartbreak and the limits
of my breath
You took the car we bought in our dreams and ran away
like criminal

And I watch your face fades into the death or the
Saturday's sunset,
And I let you escape once to consider my rising **revival**

Thank you for the sleepless nights and battered tattoos
on my grieving heart

Ronella Hope Segaya, beWITCHed

Thank you for the ironed lines and historical phrases
from the start

Ronella Hope Segaya, beWITCHed

On The Corner of Your Vigilance

Torture the endless night fevers; keep them running coming back for more;
Kiss a stranger in a nearby bar and throw up under the streetlights.
Make it red wild, stay alive, and breathe in the smell of the lonely shore;
Drive in stolen white cars, boycott road signs, sadness kills but truth fights.
Exhaling too loud, the whole town can hear you talking to the walls.
Enough of the pains, hurry buy a ticket to a foreign land,
Care no more, change your cell phone number, start rejecting wary phone calls.
Need not to sleep on men's bed to satisfy you, all you need: your hands
Find real love on corners of your vigilance; heart remain breakable,
But never in the same hand twice, my darling you deserve something more
Sometimes your self-intentions and flash emotions are mistakable,
Try to avoid dropping your wobbly knees again to the marbled floor.

The daylight never stays so is the numb darkness of the night either,
Even yourself change your peaceful mind just like your rude country's weather.

Ronella Hope Segaya, beWITCHed

Like Me

Do you regret like me?
Take the blame like me,
But never say sorry for being transparent like me
Give your fucking self away like extra change like me,
Promise your love the perfect world that you can't even
give yourself like me

Kiss the pain like me
Sleep on streets like me
Give the sky a middle finger every night like me,
Just to cry on former favorite corners of this town like
me
Cross your fingers, dance on parking lots of your careless
neighbors like me

Bite your tongue like me
Tell a lie like me
Say that you would never fall in love again like me
Just to drop your shitty heart on rocky roads like me
Try to pick them up and glue the pieces back like me

Write your words like me
Keep a pen like me,
Kiss strangers on the stones of midnight shores like me,
Let go of the promises you know that will never be filled
like me
Turn your heart to steel and learn to play like me

Open your legs like me
Welcome them like me

Ronella Hope Segaya, beWITCHed

Try not to attach some strings you can't pull off like me
Try to avoid the meteors of heartbreak like me
Just so you wouldn't have to be like me

Ronella Hope Segaya, beWITCHed

...And when there was no one
else that could close the wound
caused by my blind description
of love, I turned to you and I realized
that no man could ever love me more than you do

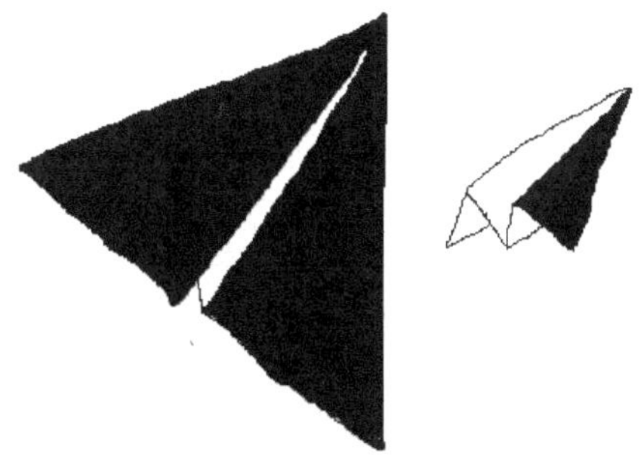

Ronella Hope Segaya, beWITCHed